HABITATS OF THE WORLD
SANDY SHORES
ALISON BALLANCE

Dominie Press, Inc.

The Coast

The coast is where the land meets the sea. The coast changes all the time, as the **tide** goes in and out. Plants and animals that live on the coast have to cope with salt water.

Sandy Beaches and Mudflats

Sandy beaches are **common** on the coast. They are soft shores. **Mudflats** are also soft shores. Mud and sand are difficult to live on because they move all the time.

Mangroves

Mangroves are trees that can grow in salt water. They trap mud around their roots and form **swamps**. Mangroves also have special roots, which stick out above the mud to help the trees draw **oxygen** from the air.

Shellfish

Many kinds of shellfish can live on sandy beaches, as long as they are always covered by water. Shellfish dig **burrows** in the sand so they don't get washed away by waves. When they die, their shells wash up on the beach.

Oystercatchers

Oystercatchers lay their eggs on a part of the beach where they won't be washed away by big waves. They feed on **sand hoppers**, which are small beach fleas. Sand hoppers live in damp sand and piles of rotting seaweed that has washed up on the beach.

Turtles

Female turtles live in the sea, but they come **ashore** to lay their eggs. They dig deep holes in the sand and lay hundreds of eggs. When the baby turtles hatch, they have to dig their way out of the sand. Then they have to run down to the water.

Estuaries

An **estuary** is where a river runs into the sea. Like mangrove swamps, estuaries are usually muddy. At low tide, the estuary looks like a mudflat. At high tide, the mudflat is covered by water.

Mudskippers

Mudskippers live in estuaries. At high tide, the mudskippers hide in burrows in the mud. They come out at low tide to feed on tiny plants that grow on the mud.

Sand Dunes

Sand dunes form when sand builds up at the top of a beach. Wind blows the sand around, so the shape of the sand dunes is always changing.

Penguins

Yellow-eyed penguins go out to sea each morning to fish. They come back to land in the evening. They have to walk across beaches and climb sand dunes to reach their nests. Yellow-eyed penguins are found only in New Zealand.

Surf Beaches

A surf beach has very big waves. The big waves make animal life on a sandy beach more difficult. People enjoy surfing and playing in the waves. Sandy beaches, mudflats, and sand dunes are interesting places that are always changing.

GLOSSARY

ashore: On dry land

burrows: Holes in the ground dug by animals and used for shelter

common: Something that happens or is found a lot

estuary: The mouth of a river where it meets the sea, affected by the tide

mudflats: Pieces of muddy land left uncovered at low tide

oxygen: The part of the air that we use when we breathe

sand hoppers: Small beach fleas that live in damp sand and rotting seaweed

swamps: Wooded areas of wetlands covered by water

tide: The daily rise and fall of the sea

INDEX